C#: The No-Nonsense Guide

Learn C# programming within 12 Hours!

CYBERPUNK UNIVERSITY

Disclaimer Notice:

Please note the information contained within this document is for educational and entertainment purposes only. Every attempt has been made to provide accurate, up to date and reliable, complete information. No warranties of any kind are expressed or implied. Readers acknowledge that the author is not engaging in the rendering of legal, financial, medical or professional advice.

By reading this document, the reader agrees that under no circumstances are we responsible for any losses, direct or indirect, which are incurred as a result of the use of information contained within this document, including, but not limited to, —errors, omissions or inaccuracies.

Table of Contents

Hour 0: Introduction to C# and .Net Framework

If you are looking forward to taking up programming seriously, you have found the right book to help you get started. This book is the right first step into programming with C# and everything .NET and is an all-round introduction for a journey into learning modern programming and software development technologies in general.

While it is a focused and simplified programming guide, C#: The No Nonsense Guide lays bare the fundamental principles and important concepts of programming, which have not changed much over the past two decades. Even if C# is not the language you wish to pursue in the future – whether as a hobbyist or a professional – this is still a great book to get introduced to programming to understand what it is before moving on to another language. This is because this book shows and teaches you how to write computer programs that solve practical algorithmic problems.

Good programming skills are formed during the initial learning of the use of various data structures and implementation of algorithms. No matter how improbable it may look, the basic principles of designing and writing computer programs have not changed much since the first object oriented programs were written in the late 1980s.

In teaching you to think algorithmically, this book will help you learn to divide the problem you want the computer to solve into a series of steps that are ach solvable, then learn to select the appropriate data structures that you can use to write top-notch programming code that solves the problem in question. This is the only way you can become an exceptional programmer.

Once you acquire the basic programming skills in the next 12 chapters, you will be able to easily learn any other programming language, no matter the technologies it is built upon. These languages include HTML5, JavaScript, ASP.NET, REST, Python, C++, Ruby, and many others.

C# and .NET Framework

C# (pronounced C-sharp) is a modern programming language developed Anders Hejlsberg and his team during the development of .NET Framework at Microsoft. The language was approved by the International Standards Organization (ISO) and the European Computer Manufacturers Association (ECMA).

It is maintained by Microsoft Corporation in collaboration with the .NET platform used for the development of software applications such as office applications, web applications, websites, desktop and mobile applications, games, and many other types of programs. C# is a high level language at par with languages such as C++ and Java, and to some extent, languages like C, VB.NET, and Delphi.

All programs developed in C# are object oriented. This means that they are made up of a set of definitions in classes that have methods, and the methods are made up of program logic or the instructions which the computer can understand and execute.

C# is among the most popular programming languages today as it is used by millions of developers around the world. This is largely because C# is developed by Microsoft as a part of their key platform known as .NET Framework for the development and execution of applications. The language has been widely adopted by Microsoft-oriented organizations, companies, and even individual developers. C# and .NET Framework are wholly maintained and managed by Microsoft and are not available to third parties. It is for this reason that many software giants such as Oracle, IBM, and SAP use Java as their primary programming language to develop their own software programs.

Microsoft distributes the C# language together with the Common Language Runtime (CLR), an environment on which the programs are executed. The CLR is a part of the .NET Framework platform which includes the CLR, compilers, a bundle of standard libraries that provide basic functionality, debuggers, and a bunch of other tools and essentials. Thanks to the versatility of the CLR, programs developed with C# are not only portable, they also run with little or no changes when used on different hardware platforms and even operating systems.

While C# programs are typically developed for MS windows OS, CLR and .NET Framework is supported on modern mobile platforms and other portable devices such as Windows 10 tablets. As a result, programs developed using C# can be seamlessly run on FreeBSD, Linux, Android, Mac OS, and other operating systems and devices that support the free .NET Framework dubbed Mono (www.mono-project.com).

C# vs Java?

We could a whole book discussing the difference between C# and Java, but one thing that will stand out the most is that Java is C#'s most formidable competitor. However, C# is undisputedly better. It is more powerful, has richer content, more diverse capabilities, and is simply better engineers. The program, as pointed out above, is easy to learn and is distributed with a free integrated environment that comes highly convenient and time-saving.

Why C#?

There are many reasons why learning to write computer programs in C# is a great idea. First off, C# is a simple and easy to learn language unlike C and C++. The language syntax is very natural and can be understood even by beginners in the world of programming. Many companies and educational organizations still use C# as the introductory programming language for their learners. Besides, being a modern programming language C# is widely used by millions of programmers all over the world.

Being an object-oriented programming language, C# is a solid programming language for any serious software requirement. This is because the language can be used to develop solutions to any real-world problems. Its objects has properties and can perform actions, and because it runs on a wide .NET Framework, C# is an ideal programming language for any learner who is looking to learn programming for fun and to build a career.

The demand for C# professionals is at an all-time high, especially as Microsoft commands over 90.5% of the computer operating system market. There is just too huge a demand for C# programmers and .NET specialists and there is never a better time for someone studying to enter the market as a service provider than now.

Here are the top reasons why C# is a widely used professional programming language:

- It is a modern, general-purpose programming language
- It is object and component oriented.
- It is a structured language that is easy to learn.
- It has a rich collection of libraries that can be used to produce efficient programs.
- It can be compiled on a wide range of different computer platforms.

While C# was designed and developed to closely follow the construct of traditional high-level languages such as C and C++, it is an object oriented programming language with a strong resemblance with Java. The same strong programming features that make Java endearing to millions of programmers around the world are present in C#. The top features include:

• Standard Library	• Assembly Versioning
• Indexers	• Delegates and Events
• LINQ and Lambda Expressions	Management
• Boolean Conditions	• Integration with Windows
• Automatic Garbage Collection	• Properties and Events
• Simple Multithreading	• Easy-to-use Generics
	• Conditional Compilation

If you are a good programmer, you will appreciate that the language you use to write your code is not as significant as knowing how to program. Whatever the technology or language you need, you can master it quickly if you already know the technical elements of creating computer programs in any OOP language. This book will not only introduce you to the .NET framework, it will also teach you the fundamentals of programming and help you learn how to think algorithmically and discover the principles on which good computer program development is built upon.

About the Cyberpunk University

This eBook is structured into 12 practical chapters that take roughly an hour to do. We have designed the content of the book to be easy to follow for both complete beginners to programming and those with knowledge of other programming languages as well as beginners to Linux and Linux gurus.

Cyberpunk University is committed to producing content that helps learners discover their coding skills and to learn processes that make it easy for them to think of solutions to daily human problems. Many other programming and DIY books are coming in the future so be sure to check our catalog and get the chance to learn even more ways to write programs in different languages that computers can understand and act upon.

Hour 1: C#, .Net Environment, and a Hello World! Program

In the introductory chapter of this book, we looked at what C# is and sought to understand why it has grown to become the celebrity it is, and the reasons it is one of the best languages to study programming today. You already know that this OOP language is used to create applications for .NET framework. Before we can venture further and learn how to create programs on this platform, we must first understand how C# relates to the .NET Framework.

1.1 The Microsoft .NET Framework

Microsoft distributes the C# language development environment as a part of Microsoft .NET Framework platform and not as a standalone product. The .NET Framework (pronounced dot net) is essentially an development environment you can use to develop and execute programs written in languages compatible with the framework such as managed C++, VB.NET, F#, COBOL, Jscript, and J#. The .NET Framework consists of:

1. Various .NET programming languages including C#, VB.NET, and others.
2. A CLR (Common Language Runtime) environment where you can execute managed code. The CLR is an application virtual machine that handles memory management, application security, and exception handling.
3. A set of development tools such as the CSC compiler. This turns C# programs into intermediate code—also called MSIL—a language that the CLR can understand.
4. A set of standard libraries such as the WCF used to connect programs through standard communication protocols and frameworks such as TCP sockets, SOAP, HTTP, and JSON and ADO.NET that allows and simplifies database access (SQL Server or MySQL).

5.   The .NET framework comes with every version of Windows OS distribution and is available in different versions. You can download it from Microsoft's website.

The latest version of .NET Framework is version 4.5 and it includes Microsoft Visual Studio 2017. Because Microsoft is determined to kill all versions of Windows prior to Windows 10, this book will be using the standard C# development platform tools that come with .NET Framework 4.5 and Visual Studio Community 2015.

1.2 C# IDE (Integrated Development Environment)

When you download Microsoft Visual Studio, it comes with the following tools that you will use in programming with C#:

- Visual Studio (VS)
- Visual C# Express (VCE)
- Visual Web Developer

You can download Visual C# Express and Visual Web Developer elements of the suite free from Microsoft's Developer website http://www.microsoft.com/visualstudio/eng/downloads/.

Armed with these tools, and the coding skills you are going to amass while studying with this book, you will be able to create all kinds of C# programs ranging from simple command-line apps to complex installable programs.

Most beginners find it easier to write the C# source code in a basic text editor file such as Notepad, Leaf or Sublime text then with a command line compiler, which comes as a part of the .NET Framework, compile the code into assemblies and execute it.

1.3 Writing C# Programs on Linux or Mac OS

The .NET Framework is a programming and program execution platform developed and maintained by Microsoft, and as such, it runs primarily on the Windows operating systems. If you own a Mac computer or use Linux, it is still possible for you to get the platform on your system but it will involve some unofficial workarounds and using an open-source version of the .NET Framework called Mono. Mono is installable on Linux and Mac computers and includes a C# compiler. You can read more about this tool and download it on Go Mono [http://www.go-mono.com/mono-downloads/download.html].

Mono was developed not only to run Microsoft's .NET applications on Linux and Mac platforms but to also bring the .NET Framework development tools for Mac and Linux developers. Mono can be run on many modern operating systems including Windows, BSD, Android, iOS, Solaris, UNIX and all distros of Linux. If you are using any of these operating systems, you might want to make sure that Mono is installed and running on your platform before you move to the next step.

1.4 Compiling and Executing a Program on Visual Studio.Net

If you do not already have Visual Studio.Net installed on your computer, go to Microsoft's website or visualstudio.com and download Visual Studio 2015 suite.

Follow the following steps to start a new project.

Step 1: Start Visual Studio from the programs menu.

Step 2: When the Visual Studio window opens, on the Menu bar, choose **File > New > Project**.

Step 3: From the templates choose Visual C# then choose Windows.

Step 4: Choose Console Application.

Step 5: Specify the name of your project, in this case, *"HelloWorld"*. Click OK to confirm.

Step 6: Your new project is created in the Solution Explorer. You can now write code in the Code Editor.

Step 7: To execute a project, save it then click on the Run button or press F5 key on the keyboard.

1.5 Writing your First Program: Hello World!

In keeping with the tradition of creating the first program as a simple Hello World! program, we are going to write the following code on the code editor of the project we created above EXACTLY as it appears.

Exercise 1: Hello World

```csharp
using System;
namespace MyExercises
{
    class HelloWorld
    {
        static void Main(string[] args)
        {
            /* Hello World! program in C# */
            Console.WriteLine("Hello World!");
            Console.ReadKey();
        }
    }
}
```

Compile and execute this code by saving it first then pressing F5 or clicking Execute on your Visual Studio development program. It should start the command prompt window and print a line that reads:

`Hello World!`

If your program does not run as expected, go back and check your code line by line and character by character to find a typo or mistake that is preventing it from running.

1.6 Compiling a C# program and running it from the command prompt

It is much easier and straightforward to compile your C# program from the command line rather than use the Visual Studio IDE, especially for the simple exercise programs like the ones you will create based on instructions in this book.

Do the following:

Step 1: Open a text editor e.g. Notepad and type the Hello World! Code in Exercise 1.

Step 2: Save the file as **HelloWorld.cs** in a location you can access with ease (Such as the Desktop).

Step 3: Open the command prompt tool and use the cd command to navigate to the directory in which you saved the **HelloWorld.cs** file.

Step 4: type **csc HelloWorld.cs** then press Enter.

The compiler will compile the code and if there are no errors, generate an executable file called HelloWorld.exe.

Step 5: Type **HelloWorld** to execute your program. You should see the output Hello World! displayed on the screen.

Note: If you get an error such as *"'csc' is not recognized as an internal or external command, operable program or batch file."*, there may be a problem with your C# installation's PATH configuration. Check your Path Environment variable and make sure that it points to a folder where the csc.exe file is located.

1.7 Program Structure of C#

A C# program is made up of the following parts:

- Namespace declaration
- A class
- Class methods
- Class attributes
- A Main method
- Statements and Expressions
- Comments

Let us break down the HelloWorld program we just created to understand all these different parts of a C# program.

using System;: The **using** keyword in the first line of the program includes the **System** namespace in the program to run. A typical C# program has multiple **using** statements.

namespace MyExercises: This is the namespace declaration. A namespace is a collection of classes. For instance, the namespace **MyExercises** that we will be using in this book contains the class **HelloWorld** and others you will create as we go along.

class HelloWorld: This is the class declaration. The name of the class is **HelloWorld** and it contains the method definitions and data the program needs to function. A typical class in C# contains multiple methods that define the behavior of the class. However, in our program, we have only defined one method called **Main**.

In future exercises, our program will begin at this point.

static void Main(string[] args): The **Main** method defined in the HelloWorld class is the **entry point** for every C# program. This method states what the class does when the program is executed.

/* Hello World! program in C# */: These are program comments. The computer will ignore all text between the comment opening symbols /* and the closing symbols */ or // and //.

Console.WriteLine("Hello World!");: The class behavior referred to in the Main method is defined in this line. In this case, it is write the string of text on the console. **WriteLine** is a method used in the **Console** class defined in the **System** namespace.

Console.ReadKey();: This line will prevent the screen from closing too fast when the program is launched from a Visual Studio.NET console.

Important Points to Note

As you begin to learn how to write code for C#, it is important to bear in mind that:

- C# is case sensitive; **using** is not the same as **Using**.
- All statements and expressions in your code must end with a semicolon (;).
- The program begins execution at the Main method.
- The program file name may be different from the class name.

Hour 2: Basic Syntax in C#

2.1 C# Syntax

Because C# is an object-oriented programming language, it is made up of various different objects that will interact with each other during the execution of its scripts through action. The action that these objects may take are what we call methods. The same kind of objects are said to be of the same type, or are referred to as objects in the same class.

For instance, in Exercise 1, consider a rectangle. It is an object with attributes that include its width and length. We can write a program that makes use of these two attributes and causes them to interact when calculating the area of the rectangle then display the results.

The basic syntax of such a program would look like Exercise 1 below:

Exercise 1: Calculating the Area of a Rectangle

```
class RectangleArea
  {
    /* variables to use */
    double length;
    double width;
    {
```

```
    length = 8.5;

    width = 10.0;

  }


  public double FindArea()

  {

    return length * width;

  }


  public void Display()

  {

    Console.WriteLine("Area: {0}", Area());

  }

}
```

Write the above code in your text editor or if you prefer the Visual Studio, on the console. Run it. Does it display the area of the rectangle?

Area: 85.0

2.1.1 The 'using' Keyword

When you write a script in C#, the first statement will always be '**using System**' as we have seen in our Hello World! Program and the in Exercise 1.

In C#, the purpose of the '**using**' keyword is to include the namespaces in the program. We have already learnt that a typical program written in C# will have multiple using statements.

2.1.2 The 'class' Keyword

The keyword 'class' in C# is used to declare a class.

2.1.3 Comments in C#

As with any other programming language, comments in C# are used to explain code to a human user. Compilers ignore all comment entries. As we saw in the previous hour, both single line and multi-line comments in C# begin with /* and terminates with */. Single line comments may also begin with //.

2.1.4 Member Variables

A variable in C# is an attribute or data member that belongs to a class and is used to store data. In Exercise 1, under the Rectangle class, we have declared two variable members: **length** and **width**, and they each can store data of type **double**.

2.1.5 Member Functions

Functions in C# refer to a set of statements that carry out a specific task or action. Member functions that belong to one class are declared within their class. In Exercise 1, we have declared two member functions under the Rectangle class: **FindArea** to calculate the area of the rectangle, and **Display** to show the result of the calculation.

2.2 Identifiers

An identifier is a name that is used to identify a variable, a class, a function, or any other user-defined element. There are three basic rules to follow when naming identifiers:

1.	It must begin with an alphabet letter. The letter can then be followed by a sequence of letters, digits, or an underscore. The first character of an identifier cannot be a number or an underscore (_) symbol.

2.   The identifier name cannot contain any symbols other than an underscore and cannot contain spaces.
3.   The identifier should not be a reserved C# keyword.

2.3 C# Keywords

Keywords are essentially words reserved in C# because they are predefined to the compiler. These are system phrases that cannot be used as identifiers. However, if you have to use a keyword as an identifier, you must prefix it with the @ character to tell the compiler that it is an identifier.

There are identifiers in C# that have a special meaning in the code context and are referred to as contextual keywords. Good examples are **get** and **set**.

Here is a list of reserved and contextual keywords that you cannot use as identifiers in C#

Reserved Keywords

abstract	do	in(generic	params	throw
as	double	modifier)	private	true
base	else	int	protected	try
bool	enum	interface	public	typeof
break	event	internal	readonly	uint
byte	explicit	is	ref	ulong
case	extern	lock	return	unchecked
catch	false	long	sbyte	unsafe
char	finally	namespace	sealed	ushort
checked	fixed	new	short	using
class	float	null	sizeof	virtual
const	for	object	stackalloc	void
continue	foreach	operator	static	volatile

decimal	goto	out	string	while
default	if	out(generic	struct	
delegate	implicitin	modifier)	switch	
		override	this	

Contextual Keywords

get	add	into	group	dynamic
set	global	orderby	remove	partial
let	partial	ascending	join	(type)
from	(method)	descending	select	
	Alias			

2.4 Data Types in C#

There are three broad types in which the variables used in C# are categorized into: **Value types**, **Reference types**, and **Pointer types**. In this section, we will briefly and generally introduce each of these data types but we will learn more about them and how to use them with variables in the next hour.

2.4.1 Value Type

Value type variables are derived from the class **System.ValueType** and can be assigned a value directly. This type of variables directly contain data e.g. **int** stores integer numbers, **char** stores alphanumeric characters, and **float** stores floating point numbers. When these value type variables are declared, the system allocates them sufficient memory to store the value type declared.

Here is a table of the value types used in C#.

Type	Represents	Range

bool	Boolean value	True or False
byte	8-bit unsigned integer	0 to 255
char	16-bit Unicode character	U +0000 to U +ffff
decimal	128-bit precise decimal values with 28-29 significant digits	(-7.9 x 1028 to 7.9 x 1028) / 100 to 28
double	64-bit double-precision floating point type	(+/-)5.0 x 10-324 to (+/-)1.7 x 10308
float	32-bit single-precision floating point type	-3.4 x 1038 to + 3.4 x 1038
int	32-bit signed integer type	-2,147,483,648 to 2,147,483,647
long	64-bit signed integer type	-9,223,372,036,854,775,808 to 9,223,372,036,854,775,807
sbyte	8-bit signed integer type	-128 to 127
short	16-bit signed integer type	-32,768 to 32,767
uint	32-bit unsigned integer type	0 to 4,294,967,295
ulong	64-bit unsigned integer type	0 to 18,446,744,073,709,551,615
ushort	16-bit unsigned integer type	0 to 65,535

2.4.2 Reference Type

Unlike Value Types, Reference Types do not have the actual data they represent stored in the variable; instead, they have a reference to the variables. What this means is that they are a reference to a particular memory location and not the value stored in that location.

In C#, you can use multiple variables to refer to the same memory location, when the data in that location is changed by one of the variables, this change will automatically be reflected in all the other variables referencing the memory location. Good examples of built-in reference types are **string**, **dynamic**, and **object** types.

String Type

The String Type is a more user-friendly name for the **System.String** class. This is a reference type variable that allows you to assign a string value to a variable. The class is derived from object type and its value can be assigned in two string literals forms: **quoted** and **@quoted**.

For example

a quoted string literal: String str = "Cyberpunk University";

a @quoted string literal: @"Cyberpunk University";

Dynamic Type

The Dynamic data type variable can store any types of values. The type of data that this kind of variable stores is checked during run time. Its syntax looks like this:

dynamic <variable_name> = value;

In an example:

dynamic mydata = 20;

Object Type

The Object Type alias Object refers to the **System.Object** class. This is the base class for every data type in C#'s **Common Type System** (CTS). You can assign an object type any type of value—value types, reference types, and even user-defined and pre-defined types. Note, however, that the type needs conversion before it is assigned to an Object Type.

Converting a value type to an object type is referred to as **boxing**. Converting an object type to a value type (the reverse of boxing) is referred to as **unboxing**.

object obj;

obj = 100; //This is boxing

User-defined reference types include: **interface**, **class**, or **delegate**. These types will be covered in the following chapters of the book.

2.4.3 Pointer Type

If you are familiar with C or C++, you have probably come across pointers. Well, the pointers in C# have the same capabilities as those in C and C++. This type of variables store the memory address of another variable type. The syntax for declaring pointer type looks like this:

```
type* identifier;
```

We will elaborate more on Pointer Types later on in the book.

Hour 3: Variables and Types Conversion

In this hour, we will learn more about variables and primitive types used in C#. We will go all-out to understand what they are and how to use them when writing code in C#. Once we cover this, we will look at the different data types used with these types and variables, characteristics and how to declare variables, as well as how values are assigned to them in C#.

3.1 What Is a Variable?

A typical computer program makes use of various values that may change constantly during program execution. The values the user enters and those the computer generates are often different and as such, there is need to let the computer know what type of data, and even values, it should reserve memory for. Variables, as introduced in the previous chapter, are essentially named temporary locations where the computer stores such data.

The computer may store variables directly in the program's operational memory (called stack) or in the dynamic memory where larger data types and objects such as arrays and character strings are stored. Primitive data types including numbers, **char**, and **bool** are referred to as value types because they store their values directly in the program stack. Reference data types including strings, objects, and arrays are called so because their values are actually addresses that point to locations in the dynamic memory where the actual data is stored.

3.1.1 Characteristics of Variables

Variables in C# are characterized by:

- **Name** (identifier) e.g. *age*;
- **Type** (type of information stored by the variable) e.g. *int*;
- **Value** (The information stored by the variable) e.g. *21*.

3.1.2 Rules of Naming Variables

In order for the compiler to allocate a memory area to information your program will process and store, you must provide a name for it. This works a lot like an identifier in that it refers to the relevant memory are where the program can retrieve and store data. C# has very rigid naming conventions that must be followed. These are:

1. A variable name must not be a reserved keyword. See previous hour for a list of reserved keywords with which you cannot name your variable.
2. A variable name may not start with a digit.
3. A variable name can contain letters A-Z, a-z, digits 0-9, as well as an underscore (_). Other symbols are not allowed.

3.1.3 Defining a Variable

The syntax for defining a variable in C# is:

```
<data_type> <variable_list>;
```

The *data_type* in this case must be one of the valid data types in hour 2.4 or any other value type variables such as **enum** and reference type variable like **class**. The *variable_list* may contain one or more identifier names separated by a comma. Here are some examples of valid variables:

```
int_ a, b, c;

float lat, lon;
```

double x, y, z;

char c1, d1;

3.1.4 Initializing Variables

To initialize a variable can also be said to assign a variable a value. This is done by naming the variable followed by an equal sign and then the constant or the value. The general syntax looks like this:

variable_name = value

Here is an example of how a variable called age is initialized:

age = 21

A variable can also be initialized by declaration. The initializer in this case consists of the data type followed by the variable name on the left side, and the value of the variable on the right side of the equal sign. The syntax looks like this:

<data_type> <variable_name> = value;

Here are some examples to help you understand better:

int x = 10, y = 12; /*initializing variables d and f*/

byte a = 192; /*Initializing a*/

double pi = 3.1416; /*declares the approximate value of pi*/

char z = 'Z'; /*declares variable z with the value 'Z'*/

As you get more practice in coding with C#, you should always keep in mind that how well your program will perform largely depends on how well the variables are initialized. Improperly initialized variables cause the program to act unpredictably or seem to work fine only to produce unexpected results.

```
class TriangleArea
{
    Static void Main(String[] args)
    {
        short b = 82;
        int h = 23;
        double Area = (b * h * 0.5);
        Console.WriteLine(b = {0}, h = {1}; Area = {2});
        Console.ReadLine();
    }
}
```

When the code in Exercise 2 is compiled and run, it should display the values of x, y, and the Area of the rectangle.

3.2 Accepting user input values

The **Console** class within the **System** namespace has the **ReadLine()** function that enables the user to enter values that it then stores in a variable. For example, in Example 2, we could have used the following line of code to enable the user enter values for b and h:

short b;

b = Convert.ToInt32(Console.ReadLine());

int h;

h = Convert.ToInt32(Console.ReadLine());

The **Convert.ToInt32()** function does exactly what its name says – it converts the data the user enters into the right data type (short for b and int for h). This is because **Console.ReadLine()** only accepts string format data.

3.3 Lvalue and RvalueExpressionsin C#:

C# has two kinds of expressions:

Lvalue is an expression that may appear on either the left or the right side of an equal sign assignment. Variables are a good example of Lvalues.

Rvalues are expressions that can only appear on the right side of the equal sign but cannot be placed on the left. A good example of Rvalues are numeric literals.

3.4 Type Conversion in C#

As we have seen in the previous hours, there are many different data types in C#. It is possible to convert from one type of data to another in a process known as casting, or more commonly, conversion. Casting takes two forms in C#: an implicit and explicit conversion types.

Implicit type casting: In this form of conversion, C# carries out the casting in a type-safe manner for instance, when converting a small integral type to a larger one or when converting from a derived class to a base class. Here is a table of possible ways primitive data types can be cast in C#:

Data type	Can be converted to
sbyte	short, int, long, float, double, decimal
byte	short, ushort, int, uint, long, ulong, float, double, decimal
short	int, long, float, double, decimal
ushort	int, uint, long, ulong, float, double, decimal
char	ushort, int, uint, long, ulong, float, double, decimal
uint	long, ulong, float, double, decimal
int	long, float, double, decimal
long	float, double, decimal
ulong	float, double, decimal

float	double

Note: There is no data loss when casting data types of smaller range to those of a larger range.

Explicit type casting: This type of conversion is done explicit by the user using a pre-defined function and it is used when there is a possibility of data loss. To carry out an explicit type casting requires a cast operator.

Exercise 3: Type Casting Application

```
class ExplicitCasting
  {
    static void Main(string[] args)
    {
      double x = 2693.04;
      int y;

      /*cast double to int*/
      y = (int)x;
      Console.WriteLine(y);
      Console.ReadKey();
    }
  }
```

What result do you get when you compile and execute the code in Exercise 3?

3.4.1 Built-in C# Type Casting Methods

There are a number of in-built conversion methods you can use in C#. Here is a table that shows what they are and a brief description for each.

Method	Description
ToBoolean	Converts a data type to a Boolean value if possible.
ToByte	Converts a data type to a byte.
ToChar	Converts a data type to one Univode character if possible.
ToDateTime	Converts an integer or string type data to a date-time structure.
ToDecimal	Converts an integer or a floating point type to a decimal type.
ToDouble	Converts a data type to a double type.
ToInt16	Converts a data type to a 16-bit integer.
ToInt32	Converts a data type to a 32-bit integer.
ToInt64	Converts a data type to a 64-bit integer.
ToSbyte	Converts a data type to a signed byte.
ToSingle	Converts a data type to a small floating point number.
ToString	Converts data to a string type.
ToType	Used when specifying the type to which a data type is converted.
ToUInt16	Converts a data type into an unsigned 16-bit integer type.
ToUInt32	Converts a data type into an unsigned 32-bit integer type
ToUInt64	Converts a data type into an unsigned 64-bit integer type.

Hour 4: Operators

Before you can start writing actual programs that can solve a user's problem, you must be acquainted with operators and what their role is. Simply put, an operator is a symbol that instructs the compiler to carry out a specific logical or mathematical manipulation on a piece of data.

Operators show the compiler how to process primitive data types and objects. They take an input from an operand and returns a value, carrying out each transformation one at a time and using one, two, or three operands.

C# has a rich arsenal of built-in operators, most of which you have come across countless times. They fall into the following categories:

1. Arithmetic (-, +, *, /, %, ++, --)
2. Logical (&&, ||, !, ^)
3. Relational (==,!=, >, <, >=, <=)
4. Bitwise
5. Assignment (=, +=, -=, *=, /=, %=, &=, |=, ^=, <<=, >>=)
6. Miscellaneous: String concatenation (+), type conversion ((type), as, is, typeof, sizeof), and others (., new, (), [], ?:, ??)

In this hour, we will briefly look at each and understand what it does but we will cover them in detail in later chapters to understand how to use them. Operators can also be categorized based on the number of arguments they can take. In this case, we will have:

1. Unary operators that take one operand.
2. Binary operators take two operands.
3. Ternary operators take three operands.

We are going to look at what these are; but first off, let use the − and + operators in a simple exercise.

Exercise 4: Operators

```
class Operators
  {
    int age = 1997 - 2017;
    Console.WriteLine(age); //Show the age
    string firstName = "Jane";
    string lastName = "Doe";
    string location = "Chinatown";
    string userID = firstName + " " + lastName + " " + age + " "
+ location;
    Console.WriteLine(userID); //Display on screen.
  }
```

4.1 Arithmetic Operators

Arithmetic operands in C# are the same ones we use in math. They perform operations such as addition, subtraction, multiplication, division and others. Here is a table summary of these operators and an example of what they do.

Operator	Description	Example
+	Adds two operands	x + y
-	Subtracts the second operand from the first	x − y
*	Multiplies both operands	x * y

/	Divides numerator by denumerator	x / y
%	Modulus operator. It returns the remainder of after an integer division	x % y
++	Increment operator. It Increases integer value by one	x++ = x + 1
--	Decrement operator. It decreases integer value by one	y-- = y - 1

When working with arithmetic operators, remember that:

- The division operator has different effects on integers and real numbers.

- Integer division by 0 causes a runtime exception **DivideByZeroException.**

Exercise 5: Operations on a square shape

```
class SquareOperators
{
    int square_Perimeter = 20;
    double square_Side = square_Perimeter / 4.0;
    double square_Area = square_ Side * square_Side;
    Console.WriteLine(square_Side); // 5.0
    Console.WriteLine(square_Area); // 16.0
}
```

4.2 Relational Operators

Relational operators, also called comparison operators, are used to compare two or more operands. Here is a tabled summary of all the relational operators supported by C#.

Suppose variable x has a value 1 and variable y has a value of 2:

Operator	Description	Example
==	Checks if the values of operands x and y are equal; if yes condition becomes true.	(x == y) is not true.
!=	Checks if the values of operands x and yare equal; if values are not equal then condition becomes true.	(x != y) is true.
>	Checks if the value of operand x is greater than the value of operand y; if yes, condition becomes true.	(x > y) is not true.
<	Checks if the value of operand x is less than the value of operand y; if yes, condition becomes true.	(x < y) is true.
>=	Checks if the value of operand x is greater than or equal to the value of operand y; if yes, the condition becomes true.	(x >= y) is not true.
<=	Checks if the value of operand x is less than or equal to the value of operand y; if yes, condition becomes true.	(x <=) is true.

4.3 Logical Operators

Logical operators take a Boolean value and returns a Boolean result (true or false). Here is a tabulation of the logical operators supported by C#.

Operator	Description	Example
&&	**Logical AND operator.** Condition becomes true if both the operands are non-zero.	(x && y) is false.
||	**Logical OR Operator.** Condition becomes true if any of the two operands is a non-zero.	(x || y) is true.
!	**Logical NOT (Negation) Operator.** Used to reverse the logical state of an operand. If the condition is true then the operator will make it false and vice versa.	!(x && y) is true.
^	**Exclusive OR.** Returns true if one of the two operands has a true value. It also returns true if the operands have different values.	x ^ y

4.4 Bitwise Operators

Binary operators work on binary representations of numeric types bit by bit. You should know by now that all data that is processed by the computer has to be converted to a binary numeral system because electronic systems use Boolean circuits. For example in the binary numeral system, the number 55 is represented as 00110111.

Here is a tabulated bitwise operator performance on binary digits 0 and 1.

x	y	~x	x & y	x | y	x ^ y
1	1	0	1	1	0
1	0	0	0	1	1
0	1	1	0	1	1

This is a table of actual bitwise operators, a brief description and an example.

Operator	Description	Example
&	Binary AND: Copies a bit to the result if it exists in both operands.	(x & y) = 12 (0000 1100)
|	Binary OR: Copies a bit if it exists in either operand.	(x | y) = 61(0011 1101)
^	Binary XOR: Copies the bit if it is set in one operand but not both.	(x ^ y) = 49 (0011 0001)
~	Binary Ones Complement: This is a unary operator that can 'flip' bits.	(~x) = 61 (1100 0011) has a signed binary number.
<<	Binary Left Shift: The left operands value is moved left by the number of bits specified on the right operand.	x << 2 = 240 (1111 0000)
>>	Binary Right Shift: The left operands value is moved right by the number of bits specified on the right operand.	x >> 2 = 15 (0000 1111)

4.5 Assignment Operators

In C#, the = symbol, a mathematical equation operator, is used to assign values to variables. The syntax for a value assignment is like this:

operand1 = literal, expression or operand2;

The operator can however be used in more ways than one. The table below summarizes the different ways the = operator is supported by C#.

Operator	Description	Example
=	Simple assignment: Assigns values from the right side operands to the left side operand	z = x + b assigns value of x + y into z
+=	Add AND assign: It adds the right operand to the left operand then assigns the result to left operand	z += x is equivalent to z = z + y
-=	Subtract AND assign: It subtracts the right operand from the left operand then assigns the result to left operand	z -= x is equivalent to z = z - x
*=	Multiply AND assign: It multiplies the right operand with the left operand and assign the result to left operand	z *= x is equivalent to z = z * x
/=	Divide AND assign: It divides the left operand with the right	z /= x is equivalent to z = z / x

	operand and assigns the result to left operand	
%=	Modulus AND assign: It takes the modulus using two operands and assigns the result to left operand	z %= x is equivalent to z = z % x
<<=	Left shift AND assign	z <<= 2 is same as z = z << 2
>>=	Right shift AND assign	z >>= 2 is same as z = z >> 2
&=	Bitwise AND assign	z &= 2 is same as z = z & 2
^=	bitwise exclusive OR and assign	z ^= 2 is same as z = z ^ 2
|=	bitwise inclusive OR and assign	z |= 2 is same as z = z | 2

Exercise 6: Compound operators

Code in this example then compile and execute it to see how the different operators affect the variables x and y.

```
class CompoundOperators
{
    int x = 10;
    int y = 7;
    Console.WriteLine(y *= 2);
```

```
    int z = y = 3;


    Console.WriteLine(z);

    Console.WriteLine(x |= 1);

    Console.WriteLine(x += 3);

    Console.WriteLine(x /= 2);

}
```

4.6 Miscellaneous Operators

There are a few other operators used in C# that do not fit in any of the five categories we have looked at so far. We will cover them here briefly.

Operator	Description	Example
sizeof()	Returns the size of a data type.	sizeof(x)
typeof()	Returns the type of a class.	typeof(x)
&	Returns the address of a variable.	&x
*	Creates pointer to a variable.	*x
? :	Conditional Expression	If Condition is true ? Then value x : else value y
is	Determines whether an object is of a certain type.	
as	Cast without encountering an exception if the cast fails.	

.	Dot, also called the access operator. It is used to access the member fields or methods of an object or class.
[]	Square Brackets are used to access elements in an array by index.
()	Brackets override the priority by which expressions are executed.
(type)	Type conversion operator is used to convert a variable from one type to another.
new	The new operator creates and initializes new objects.
??	?? is similar to ? except that it is entered between two operands to return the left operand only if it has a value that is not null; otherwise returns the right operand.

4.7 Operator Precedence in C#

Operator precedence in programming determines how terms are grouped in an expression which affects its evaluation. You learn precedence of arithmetic operators in math. Operators with the highest precedence appear at the top of the table. Operators of higher precedence are evaluated first in an expression.

Category	Operator	Associativity
Postfix	() [] -> . ++ - -	Left to right
Unary	+ - ! ~ ++ - - (type)* & sizeof	Right to left
Multiplicative	* / %	Left to right
Additive	+ -	Left to right
Shift	<< >>	Left to right

Relational	< <= > >=	Left to right
Equality	== !=	Left to right
Bitwise AND	&	Left to right
Bitwise XOR	^	Left to right
Bitwise OR	|	Left to right
Logical AND	&&	Left to right
Logical OR	||	Left to right
Conditional	?:	Right to left
Assignment	= += -= *= /= %=>>= <<= &= ^= |=	Right to left
Comma	,	Left to right

Brackets can be used to change the precedence of an operator as well as simplify expressions that are long or very complex.

Hour 5: Decision Making in C#

Just like every other computer programming language, C# has decision making structures that a programmer can use to specify one or more conditions that the program tests or evaluates. These structures have a statement or statements that are executed if the tested condition(s) are determined to be true. There may also be an optional statement or statements that are executed if the conditions evaluated return a false.

The diagram below is a general representation of a decision making structure used in most programming languages.

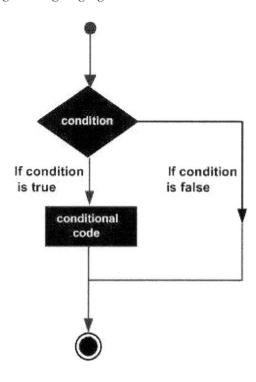

In this hour, we are going to explore the different types of decision making statements supported in C#:

5.1 'if' Statement

The **if** conditional statement is the main format of decision making in C#. When used, this statement (and if-else) cause the program to behave differently based on the results of the evaluated condition. Its syntax includes the if-clause, takes the following format:

if (expression)

{

Body of the conditional statement;

}

The condition being evaluated is in brackets is a Boolean expression between the brackets () after the **if** statement. The statement of this decision structure is locked between the curly brackets {} and may consist of one or more statements or operations.

If the expression being evaluated returns **true**, the body of the statement will be executed. It will be skipped if the result is false.

Exercise 7: Using conditional statement If

```
class ConditionIf
{
  static void Main()
  {
    Console.Write("Enter the first number: ");
    int Number_1 = int.Parse(Console.ReadLine());
```

```
Console.Write("Enter the second number: ");

int Number_2 = int.Parse(Console.ReadLine());

int largerNumber = Number_1;

if (Number_2 > Number_1)

{

  largerNumber = Number_2;

}

Console.WriteLine(" {0} is the larger number", largerNumber);

 }

}
```

5.2 'if...else' Statement

The **if...else** statement is a lot like the if statement, except that it has the else-body statement that consists of one or more expressions in curly brackets to be executed when the **if** expression to be evaluated returns a false. The syntax for this conditional statement looks like this:

```
if (expression)

{

Body of the conditional statement;

}

else

{

Body of the else statement;

}
```

Here is how this statement works: The Boolean expression after **if** is evaluated and if it returns true, the body of the conditional statement is executed and the **else** and its body statement is skipped. If the **if** statement returns false, the first body of the conditional statement is skipped and the body of the else statement is executed.

Exercise 8: if-else

```
class IfCondition
{
  static void Main()
  {
    int x = 2;
    if (x > 3)
    {
      Console.WriteLine("x is greater than 3");
    }
    Else
    {
      Console.WriteLine("x is not greater than 3");
    }
  }
}
```

5.3 Nested "if" Statements

In many cases, you will need to use programming logic that requires to be represented by multiple **if** decision making structures contained inside each other. These are what we call **nested if** or **nested if-else** structures. In such a structure, every **else** clause in the structure will correspond to the closest previous **if** clause. It is a good practice, however, not to nest more than three **if** statements.

5.4 Sequence of "if-else-if-else-..."

In the course of practicing to use the **if** and **nested if** control statements, you will find the need to use a sequence of **if** structures that use the **else** clause as a part of another **if** statement. You will discover that using the else... if statement as we have learnt so far will cause the code to be pushed too far to the right. In such a situation, it is a good practice to use **if else** as in this example.

```csharp
char score = '';

if ()

{

Console.WriteLine("A");

}

else if ()

{

Console.WriteLine("B");

}

else if ()

{

Console.WriteLine("C");

}
```

```csharp
else if ()

{

Console.WriteLine("D");

}

else if ()

{

Console.WriteLine("E");

}

Else

{

Console.WriteLine("N/A");

}
```

5.5 "switch-case" Statement

The decision making control statement **switch** selects a part of the program code to execute based on the result of a calculation of a particular expression, often of an integer type. This statement takes the following format:

```csharp
switch (selector)

{

case value1:

statements;

break;
```

```
        case value2:

        statements;

        break;

        // ...

        default:

        statements;

        break;

    }
```

This control statement is made up of a **selector** expression that returns the resulting value such as a **number** or a **string**. The switch operator essentially compares the result from the selector to the rules defined in the **case labels** within the body of the switch structure. When a match is found within the **case label**, the corresponding structure will be executed and if no match is found, the **default** statement will be executed if it exists.

It is also appropriate to use multiple labels when executing the same decision making structure in more than a single case. This is best illustrated in a simple exercise.

Exercise 8: Using Multiple Labels in a Switch Statement

```
class SwitchStatement
{
  int num = 10;
  switch (num)
  {
    case 1:
```

```
        case 4:
        case 6:
        case 8:
        case 10:
        Console.WriteLine("This is not a prime number!"); break;
        case 2:
        case 3:
        case 5:
        case 7:
        Console.WriteLine("This is a prime number!"); break;
        default:
        Console.WriteLine("This is an Unknown number!"); break;
    }
}
```

5.6 Best practices when using "switch-case"

- When using the **switch** statement, place the default statement at the very end of the structure to make it easier to read the code.
- Place the **cases** that handle the most common situations at the top of the structure. Those that handle rarely occurring situations should be placed at the end.
- If the values of the **case** labels are integers, it is recommended that you arrange them in an ascending order. Sort them alphabetically if they are of the **character** type.
- Make it a habit to use a **default** block that handles all situations that the normal operation of the program cannot handle.

5.7 The ? : Operator as a statement

We were introduced to the conditional operator **?** **:** in the previous hour. This operator can also be used in place of the **if...else** statement in the following format:

Expression1 ? Expression2 : Expression3;

Here is how the value of the ? expression is determined: **Expression1** is evaluated and if it is **true**, then **Expression2** is evaluated and is made to represent the entire ? expression. If **Expression1** is false, then Expression3 is evaluated and its value is made the new value of the expression.

Hour 6: Loops in C#

In computer programming, loops are used in situations where a program is required to execute a block of code more than once. Statements in a looped code are executed sequentially, the top statement being first, followed by the second below it, and so on.

Different programming languages offer different control structures that the programmer can use to create simple to complicated execution paths. In C#, we have four types of loops that follow the general form of loop statements in most OOP languages. They are **while**, **for**, **do**, and **nested** loops.

6.1 While Loop

A **while** loop statement repeatedly executes a particular statement as long as a pre-defined condition is true. This means that the loop will stop when the condition being tested returns a false. The syntax of a **while** loop statement in C# looks like this:

```
While (condition)

{

statement;

}
```

In this syntax, the **condition** may be an expression which returns a zero value as **false** and any non-zero value as **true**. The statement could be a single statement or a block of statements. When the condition being tested returns a false, the program control will skip the statement to execute the line immediately below the loop.

Exercise 9: While Loop

```
class MyProgram
{
  static void Main(string[] args)
  {
  /* definition of local variable */
    int x = 1;


    while (x < 10)
    {
      Console.WriteLine("value of x: {0}", x);
      a++;
    }
    Console.ReadLine();
  }
}
```

What happens when you compile and execute the above code? It should print the values of x starting at 1 incrementally till 9 then it stops.

6.2 For Loop

In most object-oriented programming languages, the **for** loop is an iteration control structure that is used to efficiently write loops that need to be executed a specific number of times. Its syntax in C# takes the following format:

```
for ( init; condition; increment )

    {

    statement;

    }
```

Here is how the for loop flow control works:

- The init step, right after the **for** statement is executed only once first. This is a very important step because it is responsible for the declaration and initialization of all loop control variables. You do not need to insert a statement at this point but there must be a semicolon right after it.

- Next is the condition to be evaluated. If the condition is evaluated and it returns **true**, then the body of the loop will be executed. However, if it returns **false**, the body of the loop will not be executed and the program flow control will skip it to the next statement after the **for** loop.

- If the condition above returns **true** and the **for** loop statement is executed, the flow control will skip back up to the increment statement. This is where any loop control statements are updated and can be left blank, provided that there is a semicolon right after the condition.

- At this point, the condition will then be evaluated again. If it returns **true** again, the loop will execute all over and the process repeats. This will go on until the condition being tested returns a **false**, after which the body statement of the loop will be skipped and the **for** loop terminates.

Exercise 10: The for loop

```
class ForLoop
{
    static void Main(string[] args)
    {
        /* the for loop execution */
        for (int x = 10; x < 20; x = x + 1)
        {
            Console.WriteLine("value of x: {0}", x);
        }
        Console.ReadLine();
    }
}
```

What result does the code in exercise return when you compile and run it?

6.3 Do...While Loop

The **while** and **for** loops test a condition at the start of the loop before iterating a statement of code, but the do...while loop is a bit different. This iteration structure checks the condition at the end of the loop. It is quite similar to the while loop except that it must execute at least once. Its syntax takes this format:

```
do
{
    statement;
```

```
}while( condition );
```

As you can see in the syntax above, the conditional expression of the **do...while** loop is at the end of the loop, meaning that the loop statements will be executed before the condition is tested. Should the test condition return true, the program's flow control will jump back to **do**, and the statement or block of statements will be executed again before the loop condition is tested after **while**. This process will repeat until the test condition returns a false, after which the loop will break.

Exercise 11: Do... While loop

```
class Program
{
  static void Main(string[] args)
  {
    /* local variable definition */
    int x = 10;
    /* do loop execution */
    do
    {
      Console.WriteLine("value of x: {0}", x);
      x = x + 1;
    } while (x < 20);
    Console.ReadLine();
  }
}
```

6.4 Nested Loops

In C#, it is possible for you to use a loop inside another loop. For instance, a nested for loop structure would have a syntax like this:

```
for ( init; condition; increment )

{

        for ( init; condition; increment )

        {

                statement1;

        }

        statement2;

}
```

For a **nested while** loop statement, the syntax would take this format:

```
while(condition)

{

        while(condition)

        {

                statement1;

        }

        statement2;

}
```

The syntax for a nested do…while iteration statement in C# would take this syntax form:

```
do

{

    statement1;

    do

    {

        statement2;

    }while( condition1 );

}while( condition2 );
```

As you can see in the syntax examples above, nesting loop statements pretty much retains the format and characteristics of the original iteration structure. An important point to note about the nested loops is that you can fit any type of loop inside another type of loop. For instance, you can have a **do…while** loop nested inside a **for** loop, or even nest a for and **do…while** loops inside a **while** loop.

Exercise 12: Using nested loops to find prime numbers between 2 and 100.

```
class NestedLoop
{
    static void Main(string[] args)
    {
        int x, y;
        for (x = 2; x < 100; x++)
        {
            for (y = 2; y <= (x / y); y++)
            if ((x % y) == 0) break;    // if factor found, not prime
```

```
    if (y > (x / y))
    Console.WriteLine("{0} is a prime number", x);
  }
  Console.ReadLine();
 }
}
```

6.5 Loop Control Statements

The operation of a loop structure is quite predictable and straightforward: when a condition is tested and met, a statement will be iterated. When the condition is tested and it returns a false, then the loop statement block will not be executed. However, you can use a loop control statement to alter the execution sequence of a loop. When the program execution terminates a loop, all the objects that were created in that particular scope are lost.

There are two loop control statements in C#: **Break** and **Continue**.

6.5.1 Break Statement

The **break** loop control statement terminates a loop or switch structure then transfers the program execution to the statement that immediately follows it. When using nested loops, the **break** statement is used to stop the execution of the innermost loop and to transfer program execution to the next line after the statement block. The syntax for **break** is simply:

    break;

Exercise 13: Using the Break statement

```
class LoopBreak
{
  static void Main(string[] args)
```

```
{
    int x = 10;
    while (x < 20)
    {
        Console.WriteLine("value of x: {0}", x);
        x++;
        if (x > 15)
        {
            /* terminate the loop using break statement */
            break;
        }
    }
    Console.ReadLine();
}
}
```

6.5.2 Continue Statement

The **continue** loop control statement is used when you wish to skip the remaining part of a loop structure body then immediately re-test the loop condition before resuming the reiteration. The **continue** statement works a lot like the break statement except that instead of forcing the loop to terminate, it initializes the next iteration of the loop, skipping any lines of code not yet executed. Its syntax is:

continue;

Exercise 13: The Continue statement

```
class ContinueStatement
{
  static void Main(string[] args)
  {
    int x = 10;
    do
    {
      if (x == 15)
      {
        /* skip the iteration */
        x = x + 1;
        continue;
      }
      Console.WriteLine("value of x: {0}", x);
      a++;
    } while (x < 20);
    Console.ReadLine();
  }
}
```

When using the **continue** statement with the **for** loop, the condition test and the increment parts of the loop will execute. However, with the **while and while…do** loops, the continue statement will cause the program to pass the conditional test.

6.6 Infinite Loop

An **infinite** loop is a type of loop whose condition never returns a **false**. In most cases, the **for** loop is used to implement an infinite loop. This is because none of the three expressions that me up the **for** loop are actually required and the loop can be implemented without them. This leaves the conditional expression empty and causing the program control to endlessly iterate the loop statements.

Exercise 14: Infinite loop

```
class InfinityLoop
{
    static void Main(string[] args)
    {
        for (; ; )
        {
            Console.WriteLine("This never ends.");
        }
    }
}
```

When there is no conditional expression in the loop, the program control assumes it to be true. You may include the initialization and the increment portions of the expression but traditionally, programmers use the **for(;;)** structure to show that the loop is infinite in nature.

Hour 7: Arrays in C#

A collection of related elements of the same type with fixed sizes are stored sequentially in arrays in C#. While an array is essentially used to store a collection of related data, it is easier for you to think of it as a collection of a similar type of variables, stored in the computer memory at continuous memory locations.

Rather than declare individual variables such as Num0, Num1, Num3,…, Num99, you would just need to declare one variable in the array such as NumX, then use Num[0], Num[1], Num[2],…, num[99] to represent the individual variables and values in the array. To access an individual array in the array, you use an index.

Elemen t Index	0	1	2	3	4	0
An array of 5 elemen ts	Num[0]	Num[1]	Num[2]	Num[3]	Num[4]	Num[0]

In the above visual representation of an array, Num[0] would be the first element represented by the index 0 and Num[4] would be the last, represented by the index 4. Since an array occupies a contiguous memory location, and it stores data sequentially, the lowest address will correspond to the first element and the highest will correspond to the last element.

7.1 Types of Arrays

Arrays may be of different dimensions, one or two, but **one dimensional arrays** are by far the most popularly used. One-dimensional arrays that we will cover this hour are also referred to as **vectors** while **two dimensional arrays** are also referred to as **matrices**.

7.2 Declaring an Arrays and Allocating it Memory

Arrays in C# have fixed length that is set during the instantiation of the array. This length is determined by the number of elements in the array. Once the length of the array has been set, it cannot be changed during the execution of the program.

To declare an array in C#, you use the following syntax:

datatype[] arrayName;

- datatype specifies the data type of the elements in the array.
- [] defines the rank or the size of the array.
- arrayName is exactly that—the name of the array.

Here is an example of an array:

float[] prices;

7.3 Initializing an Array

When you declare an array, as we declared the prices array containing the data type float in the above example, does not initialize it in memory. You can only assign values to the array after the array variable is initialized. Because an array is a reference type of data, you will need to use the new keyword to create its instance. Here is an example of an array with 5 elements:

float[] prices = new float[5];

7.4 Assigning Values to an Array

You assign values to the individual array elements using their index numbers. Here is an example:

```
float[] prices = new float[5];

prices[0] = 12.99;
```

You can also assign values to the array during declaration. The syntax for such an operation would look like this:

```
float[] prices = {12.99, 6.15,17.00, 26.50, 11.28};
```

It is a common practice for programmers to create and initialize an array in one line of code. Here is an example:

```
float[] prices = new float[5] {12.99, 6.15,17.00, 26.50, 11.28};
```

You can also choose to omit the size of the array in the initialization phase. The syntax would look something like this:

```
float[] prices = new float[] {12.99, 6.15,17.00, 26.50, 11.28};
```

If you wish, you can copy an entire array variable into another target array variable. In this case, both the source and the target arrays will point to the same memory location.

```
float[] prices = new float[] {12.99, 6.15,17.00, 26.50, 11.28};

float[] costs = prices;
```

7.5 Default Values of an Array

So far we have learnt that before we can use an array, it has to be initialized. This means that the variable has to have a value. When you create an array, even before you assign any values, the C# compiler will implicitly initialize each element of the array with a default value. The value will depend on the type of data. For example, an **int** array will have all values set to **0** during initialization and **bool** array types will have the default value set to **false**.

7.6 Accessing Array Elements

By default, arrays are zero-based, meaning that the enumeration of the elements start at 0. The first element will have the index 0, the second 1, etc. In an array of n elements, the last element will have the index n-1.

You access the elements of an array by indexing the array name. You do this by placing the indexes of the elements in square brackets after the name of the array. For example in this array:

string [] Weekdays = new string {"Mon", "Tue", "Wed", "Thu", "Fri"};

string[] MyDay = DaysOfTheWeek[2];

It is also possible for us to iterate through an array using a loop statement. The most common iteration statement to use in such a case is the **for** loop. The syntax would look like this:

int[] arrayName = new int[10]

for (int x = 0; x < arrayName.Length; x++)

{

   arrayName[x] = x;

}

Exercise 15: Arrays

In this exercise, we will put in practice the concepts we learnt above—from declaration of arrays and assigning values to initialization and accessing array elements.

```
class ForArrays
{
  static void Main(string[] args)
  {
    int [] xyz = new int[10]; /* xyz is an array with 10
integers */
    int x,y;
    /* initialize the elements of the array xyz */
    for ( x = 0; x < 10; x++ )
    {
      xyz[x] = x + 100;
    }
    /* output the value of each element of the array */
    for (y = 0; y < 10; y++ )
    {
      Console.WriteLine("Element[{0}]    =    {1}",  y,
xyz[y]);
    }
    Console.ReadKey();
  }
}
```

What happens when you compile and run the above code?

7. 7 The foreach Loop

In exercise 15 above, we used the **for** loop to access each element in the array xyz. Another alternative to the **for** loop is using the **foeach** loop statement to iterate access to the array. Let us try this in another exercise.

Exercise 16: Using foreach to iterate through an array.

```
class ForeachArrays
{
  static void Main(string[] args)
  {
    int[] xyz = new int[10];
    int x,y;

    for (int x = 0; x < 10; x++ )
    {
      xyz[x] = x + 100;
    }

    foreach (int y in xyz )
    {
      int x = y-100;
      Console.WriteLine("Element[{0}] = {1}", x, y);


    }
    Console.ReadKey();
  }
}
```

7.8 Vital Concepts of Arrays in C#

It takes a lot of practice to fully internalize the use of arrays in C#. Before you can get to practicing, there are a few definitions and concepts you should know:

Arrays are multi-dimensional: As we say at the beginning of this hour, there are more than one dimension of arrays. As you practice and learn more about arrays, you will come across matrices and get to learn how they work.

Jagged arrays: Besides multi-dimensional arrays, C# also supports jagged arrays, which means arrays of arrays or arrays inside another array.

Arrays can be passed to functions: It is possible to pass to the function of an array by pointing to its name, without necessarily using the array index.

Param arrays: This function is used to pass unknown number of parameters to a function in an array.

The Array Class: The array class is defined in the System namespace and it is the base class to all arrays. It provides the various methods and classes that are used when working with arrays.

Hour 8: Methods as Subroutines in C#

The 'divide and conquer' approach to solving tasks may have been first popularized by Romans in 2700BC, but it is still very much alive in how we program computers to solve problems today. When writing a computer program to solve complex problems using the C# language, we apply methods to split these problems into smaller chunks or sub-problems that can be more easily defined and resolved separately compared to the original complex problem.

8.1 What is a Method?

In C#, a method is a subroutine that forms a basic part of a program. It is written to solve a certain program and eventually take the parameters and return a result. In some programming language, the subroutines that handle this kind of task are called functions or procedures.

We can define a method as a group of statements in C# that together carry out a particular task. Every functional C# program has at least one class and a method named 'Main'. To use a method, you will need to define it and call it.

The syntax of a method in C# takes this format:

<Access Specifier> <Return Type> <Method Name>(Parameter List)

{

Method Body

}

Here is a brief description of a method's various elements:

Access Specifier: Determines the visibility of the method from another class.

Return type: For methods that return a value, the return type is the data type of the value the method will return. The return type is void if the method does not return any value.

Method name: This is the unique identifier of the method. It is case sensitive and cannot be the same as any other identifier already declared in the class.

Parameter list: The purpose of parameters is to pass and receive data from the method. They are enclosed in parentheses () and refers to the type, order, and the number of parameters for the particular method. Parameters are optional for methods.

Method body: The method body between { and } are a set of instructions needed for the method to carry out a particular task.

8.2 Why Use Methods?

There are many reasons why programs in C# use methods. Most of these are straightforward, but some you will understand better as you gain more programming experience. All in all, you will discover that you cannot avoid using a method to write a computer program capable of solving a serious task.

1. Methods make up a structured program with better readable code

Whenever you create a computer program, using methods the right way is a sure approach to make your program code better structured and more readable. This makes the code easier to maintain bot by you and other people.

2. Avoid Duplicated Code

A very important reason to master the use of methods is that they go a long way to help you avoid repeating similar code. The idea of code reuse is very strong when it comes to using methods. Efficient programmers use methods to avoid having to write the same code over and over.

3. Code Reuse

Still on efficiency, methods can be used to separate chunks of code used more than once in a program. This enables the programmer to reuse the same code without copy-pasting or rewriting it. This minimizes time wastage and code repeating besides improving the structure of the program.

8.3 Declaring a Method

IN the C# language, methods are declared only between the opening { and the closing } of a class. A typical example of a method is the Main () method that we have been using in the previous exercises. For illustration, consider this hello World example.

```
public class HelloWorld

{ /*This is the opening brace of the class HelloWorld*/

static void Main(string[] args) /*This is the method declaration*/

    {

            Console.WriteLine("Hello World!");

    }

} /* Closing brace of the class HelloWorld*/
```

As you can see in the example above, access modifier for the method is **static** (some are **public**) and the type of the returned value is **void**, meaning that this method does not return a result. Its name is **Main**, and it has only one parameter: the array **string[] args**.

When a method is declared, the sequence of its elements must be maintained. The access modifier comes first, followed by return type, then the name of the method, and a list of parameters enclosed in round brackets.

Exercise 17: MaxNumber method

In this exercise, we will declare a method called MaxNumber that takes two integers and returns the larger of the two. The method's access specifier is public to make it possible to access it from outside the class MyNumbers.

```csharp
class MyNumbers;
{
    public int MaxNumber(int num1, int num2);
    {
        /* declare local variable */
        int result;

        if (num1 > num2);
        result = num1;
        else
        result = num2;

        return result;
    }
}
```

8.4 Rules for Naming Methods

Microsoft has listed a number of rules that it recommends programmers use when declaring methods:

1. Always start the name of a method with an uppercase letter i.e. MaxNumber not maxnumber
2. Apply the PascalCase rule. The rule states that each new word concatenated to the method name must start with an uppercase letter i.e. MaxNumber not Maxnumber.
3. It is recommended that the method name contain a verb, or a verb and a noun.

These rules are recommended not mandatory.

8.5 Invoking a Method

The process of executing the code contained in a method's body is called invoking the method. To call a method, simply write its name followed by round brackets and a semicolon at the end. The syntax looks like this:

```
<method_name>();
```

Exercise 18: Number calculator

In this exercise, we will call the **MaxNumber** method we declared in the exercise x above. Edit your code to look like below then compile and run it.

```
class MyCalculator
{
  public int MaxNumber(int num1, int num2)
  {
    /* declare local variable */
    int result;

    if (num1 > num2)
    result = num1;
    else
```

```
        result = num2;

        return result;

    }

    static void Main(string[] args)

    {

        /* define local variable */

        int x = 100;

        int y = 200;

        int return2;

        MyNumbers n = new MyNumbers();


        /* call the MaxNumber method */

        return2 = n.MaxNumber(x, y);

        Console.WriteLine("Max value is : {0}", return2 );

        Console.ReadLine();

    }

}
```

If you declared a method with public accessibility using a public access specifier then you can also call it from other classes using the class instance. For example, the MaxNumber method can be called from another class as we see in the following exercise.

Exercise 19: Number Calculator 2

```
class MyNumbers

{

    public int MaxNumber(int num1, int num2)
```

```csharp
{
    /* Declare local variable*/

    int result;


    if(num1 > num2)
      {
         result = num1;

      }
      else

      {
      result = num2;

      }
      return result;

      }

    }

class MyTest
{
  static void Main(string[] args)
  {
    /*Define local variable*/

    int x = 100;

    int y = 200;

    int return2;

    MyNumbers n = new MyNumbers ();

  }
}
```

```
    //call the MaxNumber method
  {
  return2 = n.FindMax(x, y);
  Console.WriteLine("Max value is : {0}", return2 );
  Console.ReadLine();
  }
}
```

What do you get when you compile and run the code in Exercise 19?

8.6 Best Practices when Using Methods

Writing good code boils down to two things: functionality and readability. As far as using methods goes, there are a number of things you need to have on your fingertips as a budding C# programmer to start shaping your coding skills into the best programming style. The five most important are:

- Each method you declare must resolve a well-defined and distinct task. This, in programming, is called strong cohesion and it involves homing the focus onto a single task.
- Give your method a good and descriptive name. The name alone should make clear what the method does.
- If possible, the method name should describe the action it performs. As mentioned earlier, you can achieve this by using a verb or a combination of a verb and noun in the method name.
- A method must have minimum dependency on the class under which it is declared and to other classes and methods.
- A method must be short. Avoid writing longer and complex methods that occupy a space larger than one computer screen.
- The functionality of the method must be logically detached if it improves the code structure and the readability of the code.
- A method should do what its name says or throw an exception. However, a method must never return an incorrect result.

Hour 9: Classes

The primary and only purpose for writing a computer program is to solve a particular problem by implementing certain data in a specified way. To create a working solution, a programmer must sketch a simplified representation of the program, some form of a model, to illustrate the program flow from start to finish. Since C# is an object-oriented program, the various concepts, tools, processes, and data can be drawn with ease, and in the process outlining the model's classes of objects.

Class, an in-built feature of C# programming language, is essentially what defines the blueprint for a data type, giving a block of data and instructions a name without defining the actual data. The object class is made up of these classes and operations that can be performed on the object. Therefore, classes are objects with methods and variables as its members.

9.1 Defining a Class

To define a class in C#, first enter the access identifier (remember this from the methods hour?) use the keyword class then followed by the name of the class you are defining, and then the class body enclosed in a pair of curly braces. Here is the general structure of defining a class:

```
<access specifier> class  class_name
{
    /* member variable */
    <access specifier> <data type> variable1;

    ...

    /* member method */
    <access specifier> <return type> method1(parameter_list)
    {
        /* method body */
    }
}
```

A class contains:

- **<access specifier>**: This is the declaration statement that specifies the access rules for the class as well as its members. If the access **specifier** is not included for a particular class type, it means that it is **internal** in nature and the default access is **private** for the members.

- **Class body**: a class has a single body, just like a method. It is also enclosed in curly brackets. The class body is made up of all the contents within the curly brackets.

- **Constructor**: A constructor is used for constructing new objects. We will discuss constructors more in-depth within the hour.

- To access the class members, use the dot (.) operator. This links the name of the object with the name of the member.

Exercise 20: Declaring a Class

```
public class MyDog;
{
  private string name = "Fluffy";

  private void Bark();
  {
    Console.WriteLine("woof-woof");
  }
  Dog myDog = new Dog();
  Console.WriteLine("My dog's name is " + myDog.name);
  myDog.Bark();
}
```

9.2 Properties, Member Functions, and Encapsulation

One of the most important and proven good practice of programming with object oriented languages is the use of properties. A property in OOP is created by declaring two methods: The first is for access (reading) and the second is for modifying (setting) values of respective properties.

Consider an example where we have a class Car, which describes a car. A car has many characteristics such as make, color, or type. To access the property make, and the corresponding modification we would do this:

```
// Getting (reading) a property

string carmake = Car.Make;

// Setting (modifying) a property

Car.Make = "Tesla";
```

In order to use a custom defined class, you must first create an object of it using the reserved keywords new combined with some constructors of the class. Using the keyword new creates an object from the class type in question.

A property is used to encapsulate the state of the class in which it is declared, that is to say to protect the class from being rendered invalid.

To manipulate the newly created class, you will then have to assign it to a variable defined in the class using the dot notation. Doing this will form and keep a connection or reference between the object (class) and the variable. The dot (.) operator we saw earlier is used to call the properties of the objects and methods associated with it as well as provide access to the fields also called member variables.

In a class, a member function can be defined as a function with its own definition or prototype within the class definition, just like any other variable.

It can operate on any object within the class in which it is a member, and it has access to all the members of the object's class.

The member attributes are actually the attributes of the object and are kept private in order to implement encapsulation. The variables are accessible only via the public member functions.

9.3 Constructors in C#

A class constructor in C# is a special member function within a class that is executed when a new object is created within that class. It can also be defined as a pseudo-method whose purpose is to initialize the memory allocated for the class object, where the non-static fields are to be stored.

The constructor has the exact name of the class but it does not have a defined return type. A constructor is called using the keyword new. By default, constructors have no parameters but if you need one with parameters, it can formally take this structure when there are modifiers and parameters to be declared:

[<modifiers>] <class_name> ([<parameters_list>])

Exercise 21: Using constructors

```
class RectangleArea
{
   private double length;   // Length of a box
   private double width;  // Width of the box
   public void setLength( double len )
   {
      length = len;
   }
}
```

```
    public void setWidth( double wid )
    {
      width = wid;
    }


    public double getArea()
    {
      return length * width;
    }
}

class RectTester
{
    static void Main(string[] args)
    {
      Rectangle Rect1 = new Rectangle();   // Declare Rect1 of type
Rectangle
      Rectangle Rect2 = new Rectangle();   // Declare Rect2 of type
Rectangle
      double area;

      // Rect1 specifications
      Rect1.setLength(12.5);
      Rect1.setWidth(7.5);

      // Rect2 specifications
```

```
    Rect2.setLength(10.0);

    Rect2.setBreadth(6.0);


    // Area of Rect1

    area = Rect1.getVolume();

    Console.WriteLine("Area of Rect1 : {0}" ,area);


    // Area of Rect2

    area = Rect2.getVolume();

    Console.WriteLine("Area of Rect2 : {0}", area);


    Console.ReadKey();
  }

}
```

Can you identify which is the class and which is the constructor? Hint: Rectangle and RecTester.

9.3.1 Visibility of the Constructors

Just like with methods and variables, you can declare constructors with pre-defined levels of visibility during declaration: **private, internal, protected internal, protected**, and **public**.

9.4 Destructors C#

As you may have guessed, destructors share a lot in common with constructors: they are practically opposites.

A destructor in C# is a special member function within a class that is executed when an object in the class goes out of scope. Just like a constructor, it has the exact name of the class except for a tilde (~) that prefixes its name. The destructor is used to release memory resources for instance when the program is exiting. This member type does not return a value, does not take any parameters, and can neither be overloaded not inherited.

The exercise below will further help you understand the concept of a destructor.

Exercise 22: Using destructors

```
class SquareArea
{
    private double length;    // Length of the square
    public Square();          // This is the constructor
    {
        Console.WriteLine("Object created");
    }
    ~Square() // This is the destructor
    {
        Console.WriteLine("Object deleted");
    }

    public void setLength( double len )
    {
        length = len;
    }
}
```

```csharp
public double getLength()

{

    return length;

}


static void Main(string[] args)

{

    Square square = new Square();


    // set line length

    square.setLength(6.0);

    Console.WriteLine("Area of square: {0}",square.getLength());

}

}
```

9.5 Static Members of a Class

Static members of a class are defined using the keyword static. When a member is declared **static**, it means that there will only be one copy of the member, regardless of how many objects of the class are created during program execution.

When you declare a member to be static, it means that it will exist in only one instance. We define constants using static variables because their values may need to be retrieved by invoking the class, but without creating a new instance. Note, also, that you can initialize static variables outside the member class or function as well as inside the class definition.

Exercise 23 best demonstrates how static variables are used in C#.

Exercise 23: Using Static variables in C#

```
class StaticVariables;
{
  public static int number;
  public void count();
  {
    number++;
  }
  public int getNumber()
  {
    return number;
  }
}

class StaticTest
{
  static void Main(string[] args)
  {
    StaticVariable x = new StaticVariable();
    StaticVariable y = new StaticVariable();
    x.count();
    x.count();
    x.count();
    y.count();
    y.count();
    y.count();
```

```
    Console.WriteLine("Variable    number    for    s1:    {0}",
x.getNumber());
    Console.WriteLine("Variable    number    for    s2:    {0}",
y.getNummber());
    Console.ReadKey();
  }
}
```

What do you get when you compile and run above code? Can you explain the output in reference to the variables declared in the code?

Note that it is also possible to declare a **member function** to be **static**. Functions declared to be static will be able to access static variables only. These functions, because they are declared static, are initialized and run even before the object is created. Notice how the concept is demonstrated in the exercise 24.

Exercise 24: Declaring static member functions

```
class StaticVariable;
{
  public static int number;
  public void count();
  {
    number++;
  }
  public static int getNumber();
  {
    return number;
  }
```

```
}

class StaticTest;
{
    static void Main(string[] args);
    {
        StaticVariable x = new StaticVariable();
        x.count();
        x.count();
        x.count();
        Console.WriteLine("Variable          number:          {0}",
StaticVariable.getNumber());
        Console.ReadKey();
    }
}
```

Hour 10: Strings and Text Processing

One of the most practical ways that every new programmer gets to apply the programming skills they learn in any object-oriented programming language is how to manipulate strings and text files. In C#, manipulating text characters requires that you learn about substrings, the **System.String** class, and various basic operations on text. In this hour, these are exactly what we will be learning.

10.1 What is a String?

Do you remember the type **char** we introduced at the beginning of this course? Well, in the variable type **char**, we get to assign one letter character to a variable. With strings, we get to work with a sequence of these **char** characters. Simply put, a string is an object whose value is text. This text is stored sequentially as a read-only collection of Char type of objects and it does not have a null-terminating character at its end.

10.1.1 The System.String Class

We are able to handle and manipulate strings in C# thanks to the **System.String class**. Strings are declared using the keyword **string**, which is actually an alias for **System.String** class in the .NET Framework. Here is an example code on how a string is declared in C#:

```
string greeting = "Hello World!";
```

While the **System.String** is the primary class used in manipulating text in C#, it is not the only or the universal solution for this purpose. Because it is a class, it abides by the principles of OOP which include storing data in the managed dynamic memory and its variables maintaining a reference to objects in the memory heap.

10.2 Creating a String Object

There are several ways you can create a string object:

1. Using a string class as a constructor (refer to hour 9).
2. Assigning a string literal to a string variable.
3. Calling a method or retrieving a property that returns a string.
4. Using the string concatenation operator (+)
5. Using a formatting method to convert an object or value to a string.

In Exercise 25, you will practice the different ways to create a string object in C#.

Exercise 25: Creating string objects

```
class StringProgram
{
  static void Main(string[] args)
  {
    /* Using string literal and concatenation */
    string FirstName, LastName;
    FirstName = "Bill";
    LastName = "Gates";

    string FullName = FirstName + LastName;
    Console.WriteLine("Full Name: {0}", FullName);

    /* using string constructor */
    char[] MyLetters = { 'H', 'e', 'l', 'l','o', 'W', 'o', 'r', 'd','!' };
    string greetings = new string(MyLetters);
```

```
    Console.WriteLine("Greetings: {0}", greetings);


    /* Using a method that returns a string */
    string[] Msg = { "Hello", "From", "Cyberpunk", "University" };
    string Msg = String.Join(" ", Msg);
    Console.WriteLine("Message: {0}", Msg);


    /* convert from a different data type */
    DateTime waiting = new DateTime(2017, 03, 19, 23, 21, 17);
    string Message = String.Format("Message sent at {0:t} on {0:D}",
waiting);
    Console.WriteLine("Message: {0}", Message);
  }
}
```

Compile the code in the above exercise and run it. Notice the different strings the console will print? Do you understand the methods used to declare the strings well enough to try and use them in your own exercise?

10.3 Reading and Printing Strings to the Console

When the user enters a string of characters, they are read using the **System.Console** class. The syntax reads like this:

```
string MyName = Console.ReadLine();
```

For this illustration, the method **ReadLine()** is used to process the data input from the user. This process waits for the user to enter a value and press the return key (Enter) then it assigns the values read from the keyboard to the string variable called **MyName**.

The same **System.Console** is what we use to output standard strings using a syntax such as this:

Console.WriteLine("Enter your name: " + MyName);

The **Write.Line()** method used in printing the string value to be output will display the message "Enter your name: " then the value of the **MyName** variable. At the end, this method adds a new line character. To print this text without the new line, which means that all messages will appear on one line, you can use the **Write(…)** method.

10.4 Properties of the String Class

The System.String class or plainly the string class has these two properties:

1. **Chars**: This property is used to get the **Char** object (or the text character) at a specified position within the current string object.

2. **Length**: The length property is used to get the number of characters that a string object is made up of.

Exercise 26: Using Char in string

Enter the following code in your text editor then compile and run to see how the **Length** property is used in the string class. Can you write your own that makes use of the **Char** property?

```
class StringMessage;
string MyMessage = "This is message for the entire world.";
Console.WriteLine("My message = {0}", MyMessage);
Console.WriteLine("MyMessage.Length = {0}", MyMessage.Length);
for (int i = 0; i < MyMessage.Length; i++);
{
  Console.WriteLine("My message[{0}] = {1}", i, MyMessage[i]);
}
```

10.5 Methods of the String Class

There are many methods that you will get to know and use to help you manipulate string objects. Below is a tabulation of the most commonly used methods, some of which we have already used in previous exercises.

Method	Description
public static int Compare(string str1, string str2)	Compares two string objects then returns an integer value indicating their relative position in the sort order.
public static string Concat(string str0, string str1)	Concatenates two string objects.
public bool Contains(string_value)	Returns a value showing whether the String object occurs within the specified string.
public static string Copy(string str1)	Creates a new String object that has the same value as the specified string.
public bool EndsWith(string_value)	Used to determine whether the end of a string object matches the specified string.
public bool Equals(string_value)	Determines whether the value of the current String object equals that of the specified String object.
public static bool Equals(string str1, string str2)	Determines whether the two String objects have the same value.
public static string Format(string format, Object arg)	Replaces a format item or items in a string with the string representation of the specified object.
public bool StartsWith(string value)	Checks to see whether the beginning of the string instance matches the specified string.
public int IndexOf(string_value)	Returns the index of the first occurrence of the specified string in this instance.

public int IndexOf(string value, int startIndex)	Returns the index of the first occurrence of the string in the current instance, beginning the search at the specified character position.
public int IndexOfAny(char[] anyOf)	Returns the index of the first occurrence in this instance of any character in a specified array of Unicode characters.
public string Insert(int startIndex, string_value)	Returns a new string object in which the current string value is inserted at the specified index position.
public static bool IsNullOrEmpty(string value)	Shows whether the specified string is an empty string or a null.
public int LastIndexOf(char_value)	Returns the index position of the last occurrence of the specified character within the string object.
public int LastIndexOf(string value)	Returns the index position of the last occurrence of the specified string within the string object.
public string Remove(int startIndex)	Removes all the characters in the string instance, starting at a specified position through the last position, then returns the string.
public string Remove(int startIndex, int count)	Removes the specified number of characters in the current string beginning at a specified position and returns the string.
public string Replace(char oldChar, char newChar)	Replaces all occurrences of the character in the current string object with the specified character then returns the new string.
public string ToLower()	Returns a copy of the string with all characters converted to lowercase.

| public string ToUpper() | Returns a copy of the string with all characters converted to uppercase. |
| public string Trim() | Removes all the leading and trailing white-space characters from a String object. |

To see a complete list of the string class constructors and methods, visit the MSDN library.

Here are two exercises that will guide you on how to use methods on **System.String** class:

Exercise 27: Joining strings

```
class StringsApp
{
    static void Main(string[] args)
    {
        string[] MyPoem = new string[]{"The Dust of Snow",
        "The way a crow",
        "Shook down on me",
        "The dust of snow",
        "From a hemlock tree"};

        string str = String.Join("\n", MyPoem);
        Console.WriteLine(str);
    }
}
```

Exercise 28: Comparing Strings

```
class MyStringsApp
{
  static void Main(string[] args)
  {
    string strA = "text to test";
    string strB = "text to test";

    if (String.Compare(strA, strB) == 0)
    {
      Console.WriteLine(strA + " and " + str2 + " are the same.");
    }
    else
    {
      Console.WriteLine(strA + " and " + str2 + " are not the
same.");
    }
    Console.ReadKey();
  }
}
```

Hour 11: Creating and Using Objects

We have already established that C# is an object-oriented programming language or OOP. This essentially means that it uses objects that interact to create computer programs. OOP languages are easy to understand and modelling program structure and code fragments is very intuitive with simple logic. This hour, we get into detail on objects of C# as the basic concepts of creating object oriented programs.

11.1 What Is an Object?

The primary reason learning to write computer programs using OOP languages is that the objects in this context are modelled after abstract concepts or real world objects. Real world objects such as a pen or a car while abstract objects used in computer programming are essentially stacks, queues, lists, and tree data structures.

Objects in C# and other OOP languages can be defined by the type of data that make up their structure, as well as how they are processed or data members and their methods. Data members are embedded in object variables which describe the state of the data and methods are tools for building the objects.

11.2 Creating and Using an Object

To create new objects based on pre-defined classes during the execution of a program, we use the operator **new**. The newly created object is typically assigned a variable from a data type that matches the class of the object. In such an assignment, the object is not copied; only the reference (address in computer memory) to the newly created object is stored in the variable. Here is an example:

```
Dog myDog = new Dog();
```

Rhe variable myDog of type Dog is assigned the newly created instance of the Dog class. While the variable myDog remains in the stack, its value, the instance of the Dog class will be strored in the managed heap.

11.2.1 Creating an Object with Set Parameters

As you gain more experience with C# programming, you will discover that it is easier to create a new object and assign them parameters at the same time rather than create it first as we did in the example above, then later in the code assign it parameters. In our example above, we would create a new object with pre-set parameters like this:

Dog myDog = new Dog("Fluff", "Dalmatian");

In this case, the object myDog represents a dog whose name is "Fluff" and it is a Dalmatian breed. We have indicated these in the object parameters between the brackets after the name of the class.

When you create a new object using the operator **new**, the compiler does two things:

1. A memory space is set aside for the new object created
2. The data members of the new object are initialized by a special method known as constructor (see hour 9).

In our example above, the initializing parameters are the constructor class's parameter.

11.2.2 Releasing an Object

One of the most important features when working with objects in C# is that you do not need to destroy objects to release the memory space they take up. This is because the .NET framework has an embedded garbage collector CLR system that cleans the memory by releasing unused objects so you do not have to. An object with no reference in the running program will be automatically released and the memory it takes up is released. This prevents potential problems and bugs in the program.

However, it is possible for you to manually release certain objects that you purposefully wish to destroy. You can achieve this by destroying the reference to it in such a manner:

```
myDog = null;
```

Note that releasing an object like this does not destroy it immediately; it basically makes it inaccessible to the running program such that the next time the garbage collector is cleaning the memory, the object will be automatically released.

11.3 Access to Fields of an Object

We have already learnt that in C#, we use the dot (.) operator to access the properties and fields of an object. The dot is placed between the name of the object and the name of the property or the field to access. However, the dot is not necessary when accessing the property or field of a class in the body of a method of the same class.

We access fields and properties of objects to assign new data and to extract data from them. We can access the property of an object just the same way as we access its field – using the keywords set and get within the definition of the property to assign and extract the values of the property respectively.

For instance, in the example above, the class **Dog** could feature properties **Name** and **Breed**. If we were to use these in an example, our code could look like this:

```
static void Main();
{
    Dog myDog = new Dog();
    myDog.Name = "Bosco";
```

```
    Console.WriteLine("The    name    of    my    dog    is    {0}.",
myDog.Name);
    }
```

11.4 Calling Methods of Objects

To call the methods of an object in C#, we use the invocation operator ()
together with the dot (.) operator. However, note that the dot is not
mandatory when the method is called within the body of another method in
the same class. To call a method, simply use its name followed by brackets ()
or if it has parameters, they will be contained within the brackets.

Exercise 29: Calling object methods

In this exercise, we call the method SayWoof of the class DogApp.

```
class DogApp;
{
  static void Main()
  {
  Dog myDog = new Dog();
  myDog.Name = "Bosco";
  Console.WriteLine("The name of my dog is {0}.",myDog.Name);
  myDog.SayWoof ();
  }
}
```

11.5 Static Fields and Methods

So far, the data members that we have covered are directly related to the instances of their classes and are implement the states of objects. In C#, there are special categories of methods and fields called static members that are associated with the data type (class) but not with the instance of the object. Static members are independent of objects and can be used without creating class instances in which they are defined.

To define a static method or field, we use the keyword static before the type of the returned method value or the field. If you will pursue programming in C# beyond the basic and intermediate, you will learn more about static fields and methods and how they are used as explained in the MSDN.

11.6 Namespaces

In C#, a namespace can be defined as a named group of classes that are related or simply a group of classes that are used in a common context or united by a common feature. Namespaces are used ti better organize the source code of a program by creating and arranging a semantic division of the classes, often in categories, to make them easier to use and manipulate.

A namespace name should always match the name of the folder, just the way the names of the independent files should match that of the classes in which they are defined. By default, a namespace explorer is visualized like a dock to the right of the integrated environment in Visual Studio, the platform on which you create C# programs.

To name an existing or a new namespace, you can do it manually using the keyword namespace preceding the full name of the namespace. Namespaces in C# should always begin with a capital letter and written in Pascal Case:

```
namespace <NamespaceName>
{
        ...
}
```

Hour 12: Exception Handling

12.1 What is an Exception?

When a problem is encountered during the execution of a program, the compiler will generate a notification pointing out the error. The response to the exceptional circumstance that arises during the running of the program provides a paradigm for detecting and reacting to the unexpected event. When this happens, the state of the program is saved, and the normal flow is interrupted and passed to the exception handler.

In C#, exceptions offer a way to transfer the control of the program to the exception handler which assesses the error or the unusual situation encountered. Exception handling is an internal mechanism that is part of the CLR (Common Language Runtime) that allows for exceptions to be thrown and caught. The handler propagates each exception to the code that handles that type of errors and it is built on four keywords:

try: The purpose of a **try** block is to identify the block of code in which a particular exception is encountered. The **try** block is often followed by one or more catch blocks.

catch: The exception handler catches the exception at the position in the program where you want to handle the problem. The keyword catch indicates that the exception has been caught.

finally: The finally block of code executes a set of statements that will throw or not throw the exception.

throw: The program throws an exception when a problem is encountered. The keyword **throw** is used in this block.

12.2 Catching Exceptions

Exceptions are considered objects in .NET. This is because it signals an event or an error not anticipated in the normal execution of the program. When an exception is raised in a block, a method will catch it using a combination of **try** and **catch** keywords or simply **try/catch**.

The **try/catch** block of code is placed around the block of code likely to generate an exception. The code around which the try/catch block is placed is referred to as protected code and its syntax will look like this:

```
try

{

        /*statements that may cause the exception*/

}

catch(ExceptionName1)

{

        /*error handling code*/

}

catch(ExceptionName2)

{

        /*error handling code*/

}

finally

{

        /*statements to be executed*/

}
```

As you can see in the code, it is possible to write several blocks of code or statements to catch different types of exceptions within the try/catch structure. This is also applicable in situations where the code may raise more than one exception in different situations.

12.3 Exception Classes in C#

Exceptions in C# are represented by classes. These classes are mainly derived from the **System.Exception** class, either directly or indirectly. Two of the most popular of these exception classes are the **System.SystemException** and the **System.ApplicationException**. The **System.SystemException** class is the base for all predefined system exceptions while the **System.ApplicationException** class supports exceptions that are generated by application programs. The exceptions that you will define while developing programs in C# will be derived from the application exception class.

Here is a table of predefined exception classes derived from the **System.SystemException** class:

Exception Class	Description
System.IO.IOException	Exception handles I/O errors.
System.InvalidCastException	Handles errors encountered when typecasting.
System.IndexOutOfRangeException	Handles errors encountered when a method refers to an array index that is out of range.

System.StackOverflowException	Handles errors encountered when there is stack overflow.
System.OutOfMemoryException	Handles errors encountered when there is insufficient free memory.
System.ArrayTypeMismatchException	Handles errors encountered when type is mismatched with the array type.
System.NullReferenceException	Handles errors encountered when deferencing a null object.
System.DivideByZeroException	Handles errors encountered when dividing a dividend with zero.

12.4 Handling Exceptions

The try/catch structure of exception handling in C# separates the core program statements from the error handling statements. In the exercise below, you will notice how the try, catch, and finally keywords are used in throwing an exception when an exception resulting from a division by zero occurs.

```
class NumberDivision
{
  int result;
  NumberDivision ();
  {
    result = 0;
  }
  public void division(int number1, int number2);
  {
    try
    {
      result = number1 / number2;
    }
    catch (DivByZeroException e);
    {
      Console.WriteLine("Exception caught: {0}", e);
    }
    finally
    {
      Console.WriteLine("Result: {0}", result);
    }
  }
  static void Main(string[] args);
  {
```

```
    NumberDivision d = new NumberDivision ();

    d.division(25, 0);

    Console.ReadKey();

  }
 }

}
```

What happens when you compile and execute the above code?

12.5 Creating User-Defined Exceptions

C# allows you to define your own exceptions and to come up with exception handling classes derived from the Exception class. In exercise 31, we will write a program that illustrates how you can create a user-defined exception handling process.

Exercise 31: Defining exceptions

```
class TempTest
{
  static void Main(string[] args);
  {
    Temperature temp = new Temperature();
    try
    {
      temp.showTemp();
    }
    catch (ZeroTempException e);
    {
      Console.WriteLine("ZeroTempException: {0}", e.Message);
```

```
        }
      Console.ReadKey();
    }
}


public class ZeroTempException
{
    Public class ZeroTempException(string message): base(message);
}


public class Temperature;
{
    int temperature = 0;
    public void showTemp()
    {
      if(temperature == 0)
        {
          throw (new ZeroTempException("Temperature is Zero"));
        }
      else
        {
          Console.WriteLine("Temperature: {0}", temperature);
        }
    }
}
```

When you compile and run the code above, it should print the error:

"ZeroTempException: Temperature is Zero".

12.6 Throwing Objects

If an exception is derived from the **System.Exception** class, whether directly or indirectly, you can use a throw statement within the catch block to throw the present object using the following syntax:

```
Catch(Exception e)

{

    ...

    Throw e

}
```

12.7 Grouping Different Error Types

Exceptions are handled in the hierarchical order in which the exceptions occur. This means that it is possible for us to catch and handle even whole groups of exceptions at the same time. Not only does the catch keyword catch the specified type of exception, but it also catches an entire hierarchy of different types of exceptions that are inheritors of the type of exception already declared in a class.

For instance, when an I/O exception (IOException is caught, all of its descendants including **EndOfStreamException, FileNotFoundException**, and **PathTooLongException** and many others will be handled when they are encountered. However, because such exceptions as **OutOfMemoryException** and **UnauthorizedAccessException** do not inherit from **IOException**, they will not be caught. As you gain more experience with C# and in particular exception handling, you will get more familiar with the exceptions hierarchy defined in the MSDN and which exceptions can catch them.

12.8 Best Practices when Handling Exceptions

While it is a good practice to structure your code to catch as many exceptions as possible, it is not possible to catch all exceptions. It is not a good practice to catch exceptions under **Exception** and all its inheritors; it is recommended that you refine your code to catch more specific groups of exceptions such as **IOException** or just a single type of exception like **FileNotFoundException**.

You should never rely on exceptions to shape the direction your code takes.

It is not a good practice to write code that relies on exceptions for expected events because throwing an exception is time consuming and affects the overall performance of the program. As we have learnt, exception handlers in C# are objects and as such, they have to be created to handle the exceptions. This means the stack trace must be initialized and the handler must be initialized to find the exception.

You should never throw exceptions to the end user.

End users find exceptions confusing and typically give the impression that the program was poorly written with bugs. Every dialog the program pops up drives the user a little crazy, no matter how well intentioned. Therefore, it is a good practice to design user-friendly and understandable error messages that offer the option to display technical information about the error.

Conclusion

If you have gone through this entire book and tried the over 30 exercises included in the 12 hours of the book, accept our well-deserved congratulations! There is no doubt that you have amassed valuable knowledge that will help you become a computer whisperer of some sort – someone who can write a program that a computer can use to solve human problems. This book has subtly taught you a lot more than just programming and data structures used in object-oriented programming; you have also mastered the algorithmic way of thinking and gained experience in solving programming problems.

If you have solved all the problems in the 12 chapters of the book in addition to mastering all the concepts and principles outlined, you can declare yourself a proficient .NET programmer. With a little studying, you will also grasp the basics and fundamental principles of developing applications for the web using HTML5, manipulating databases in SQL, and using server-side software such as WCF and ASP.NET that directly relate to .NET development platform. You have a great advantage over most programmers revolutionizing how computers work for us now.

What next?

There are a lot you still need to learn and practice before you can comfortably apply your knowledge in C# to solve world problems. We will not sugarcoat it – it will take even more effort and hard work to be proficient. It is a heavy price to pay, but considering how far you have come, it will be child's play.

There is a lot you can do from this point. This book does not cover everything, and even what it covers, it does not go deep enough to make you the best in developing programs in C#. You have laid a solid foundation with this book and there is a universe of options available to you to progress and grow. Here are a few steps you can take form this point:

- **Focus on one programming platform and study to become an intermediate then advanced developer in that field**. Most programmers choose to focus on one platform such as app development or database administration as a career path.
- **You can also choose to start building dynamic websites using HTML5, CSS, and JavaScript**. You can then explore such branches as ASP.NET Web forms or focus on developing tools and programs for mobile devices.
- **Alternatively, you can take up more serious projects such as the web market or get a job for software companies**. You will need to build your confidence a little more to apply your skills in practical software development but there is no better place to start than in the corporate world.

Good luck to you.

www.ingramcontent.com/pod-product-compliance
Lightning Source LLC
Chambersburg PA
CBHW071550080326
40690CB00056B/1625